Sanjeev Kapoor's KHAZANA

Best of Paneer

In association with Alyona Kapoor

PopulaR prakashan

www.popularprakashan.com

Published by
POPULAR PRAKASHAN PVT. LTD.
301, Mahalaxmi Chambers
22, Bhulabhai Desai Road
Mumbai - 400 026
for KHANA KHAZANA PUBLICATIONS PVT. LTD.

(4393)
ISBN: 978-81-7991-645-2

Design: Anjali Sawant
Photography: Bharat Bhirangi and Vikas Shinde

PRINTED IN INDIA
by Trident Offset Works
B-97/4, Naraina Industrial Area
Phase I, New Delhi

CONTENTS

AUTHOR'S NOTE

Paneer, cottage cheese, *chaman, chhena,* the home-made white cheese with many names, has always been a part of Indian cuisine.

In recent times *paneer* has assumed the status of a delicious, nutritious alternative to non-vegetarian food. Packed as it is with protein and all the goodness of milk, vegetarians have found that *paneer* is the perfect substitute for meat and poultry in almost any dish.

There is a reason why the English name for *paneer* is "cottage cheese": it is the simplest cheese to make at home. Unlike other cheeses, it needs no special equipment or complicated technique. Lemon juice, vinegar or a cup of whey, a piece of muslin and a strainer—everyday kitchen stuff is all that one needs to turn out delicious *paneer* in a matter of minutes.

In *Best of Paneer,* I have introduced you to a mouth-watering assortment of delectable *paneer* recipes. Try the smooth and silky Shahi Paneer, the melt-in-the-mouth Grilled Paneer with Honey-Chilli Sauce, delicious Paneer Makhni, quick and easy Paneer Bhurji, rich Paneer Piste ka Salan, and delightful *mithai* like Raj Bhog, Sandesh, among many others.

Happy Cooking!

AMRITSARI PANEER PAKORA

Ingredients

400 grams cottage cheese, cut into 1-inch cubes

½ cup Green Chutney (page 95)

2½ cups gram flour

2 teaspoons carom seeds

1 teaspoon ginger-garlic paste

1½ teaspoons red chilli powder

Salt to taste

1 tablespoon lemon juice

Oil for deep-frying

Method

1 Make a deep slit in each cube of cottage cheese without cutting through. Stuff the slit with the green chutney.

2 Mix the gram flour with one cup of water; add the carom seeds, ginger-garlic paste, chilli powder, salt and lemon juice and mix well to make a smooth batter.

3 Heat the oil in a non-stick *kadai*. Dip the stuffed cottage cheese cubes in the batter and deep-fry till golden.

4 Drain on absorbent paper. Serve hot with tomato ketchup or chutney of your choice.

TIRANGA PANEER TIKKA

Ingredients

450 grams cottage cheese

½ teaspoon red chilli powder

4 tablespoons Green Chutney (page 95)

Salt to taste

1 cup yogurt

2 tablespoons gram flour

½ tablespoon ginger paste

½ tablespoon garlic paste

4 tablespoons chopped fresh coriander

4 green chillies, chopped

1½ tablespoons lemon juice

Melted butter for basting

Method

1 Grate one hundred grams of cottage cheese and cut the remaining into one-and-a-half-inch cubes. Slice each cube into two layers without cutting through.

2 In a bowl, mix together the grated cottage cheese, chilli powder and salt.

3 Take a cottage cheese cube, spread green chutney over the first layer, and cottage cheese mixture on the second layer.

4 In a deep bowl, mix together the yogurt, gram flour, ginger paste, garlic paste, chopped coriander, green chillies, salt and lemon juice.

 Snacks

5 Add the stuffed cottage cheese cubes and mix gently so that all the cubes are evenly coated with the marinade. Set aside for about an hour.

6 Thread the cottage cheese cubes, a little apart, onto skewers and roast over a moderately hot charcoal grill for five to six minutes, basting them with melted butter once in between. You can also cook them on a hot non-stick *tawa* or griddle.

7 Serve immediately.

COTTAGE CHEESE (*Paneer*)

To make paneer, bring one litre of milk to a boil. Immediately add two tablespoons of lemon juice or vinegar and continue to boil, stirring continuously, till all the milk curdles and separates from the whey.
Drain and tie the curds up in a piece of muslin. Dip the potli in chilled water so that it cools down completely. Squeeze out the water again.
Place the paneer under a heavy weight so that all the water drains away and the paneer sets as a block.

SAUNFIA PANEER TIKKA

Ingredients

500 grams cottage cheese

½ teaspoon Lucknowi fennel seed powder

2 tablespoons gram flour

¼ teaspoon turmeric powder

½ tablespoon ginger paste

½ tablespoon garlic paste

½ teaspoon white pepper powder

Salt to taste

2 tablespoons lemon juice

½ teaspoon green cardamom powder

A few saffron threads

1 cup yogurt, drained

2 medium green capsicums, cut into 1½-inch squares

1½ teaspoons *chaat masala*

Method

1 Wash and cut the cottage cheese into one-and-a-half-inch squares of half-an-inch thickness.

2 Heat a non-stick pan. Add the gram flour and roast over a medium heat

until fragrant. Remove from heat and add the turmeric powder. Cool and transfer to a bowl.

3 Add the ginger paste, garlic paste, white pepper powder, salt, one tablespoon of lemon juice, cardamom powder, fennel seed powder, saffron and yogurt. Whisk well to make a batter.

4 Add the cottage cheese to the batter and marinate for at least an hour.

5 Preheat the oven to 220°C/425°F/Gas Mark 7.

6 Thread the cottage cheese pieces and capsicum squares alternately onto the skewers.

7 Cook in the preheated oven for three minutes on either side.

8 Alternatively, roast them in a *tandoor* or over a charcoal grill for five minutes till golden brown.

9 Remove and sprinkle with *chaat masala* and the remaining lemon juice. Serve with chutney.

HARA BHARA PANEER TIKKA

Ingredients

- 300 grams cottage cheese, cut into 1½-inch cubes
- 120 grams fresh coriander, roughly chopped
- 60 grams fresh mint, roughly chopped
- 4 green chillies, roughly chopped
- 10 garlic cloves, roughly chopped
- 1 cup yogurt
- 3 tablespoons gram flour
- Salt to taste
- 1 teaspoon *chaat masala*
- ½ teaspoon *garam masala* powder
- 1 tablespoon lemon juice
- 1 tablespoon oil

Method

1 Coarsely grind the chopped coriander and mint, green chillies and garlic.

2 Transfer to a bowl, add the yogurt, gram flour, salt, *chaat masala*, *garam masala* powder and lemon juice and mix well.

3 Stir in the oil; add the cottage cheese and mix well so that all the pieces are well-coated with the mixture.

 Snacks

4 Set aside to marinate for about half an hour.

5 Heat a non-stick *tawa*. Thread the cottage cheese pieces, one-inch apart, onto skewers and grill turning from time to time, for about fifteen minutes, or till evenly cooked on all sides.

6 Serve hot with onion rings and lemon wedges.

PANEER CAPSICUM PAKORE

Ingredients

250 grams cottage cheese,
cut into 1-inch squares

4 medium green capsicums, seeded
and cut into 1-inch squares

125 grams fresh coriander, chopped

125 grams fresh mint leaves, chopped

2 green chillies, chopped

½ tablespoon lemon juice

Salt to taste

2 teaspoons *chaat masala*

1 teaspoon red chilli powder

Oil for deep-frying

Batter

½ inch ginger, chopped

2 garlic cloves, chopped

2 green chillies, chopped

1 cup gram flour

3 tablespoons cornflour

½ teaspoon baking powder

¼ teaspoon turmeric powder

1 teaspoon red chillies, crushed

Salt to taste

1 tablespoon lemon juice

1 tablespoon oil

Method

1 For the green chutney, grind together the fresh coriander, mint leaves and green chillies to a fine paste. Add the lemon juice and salt to taste.

2 For the batter, grind together the ginger, garlic and green chillies to a fine paste.

3 Mix together the gram flour, cornflour, baking powder, turmeric powder, crushed red chillies, ginger-garlic-green chilli paste and salt in a bowl.

4 Add the lemon juice and oil, and mix. Add half a cup of water to make a thick batter.

5 Spread the green chutney on either side of the cottage cheese squares. Sandwich each cottage cheese square between two capsicum squares.

6 In a bowl, mix the *chaat masala* and chilli powder. Set aside.

7 Heat sufficient oil in a non-stick *kadai*. Dip the sandwiched cottage cheese squares in the batter and deep-fry till golden brown.

8 Drain on absorbent paper. Cut into halves and place on a serving plate.

9 Sprinkle the *chaat masala* and the chilli powder mixture, and serve hot.

PANEER KE TINKE

Ingredients

300 grams cottage cheese, cut into 1-inch cubes

3 teaspoons oil

2 tablespoons gram flour

¾ cup drained (hung) yogurt

1 teaspoon roasted cumin powder

3-4 black peppercorns, crushed

½ teaspoon roasted crushed dried fenugreek leaves

½ teaspoon turmeric powder

½ teaspoon *garam masala* powder

5 teaspoons lemon juice

Salt to taste

A few saffron threads (optional)

1 medium onion, cut into 1-inch pieces, layers separated

1 medium green capsicum, cut into 1-inch pieces

1 medium red capsicum, cut into 1-inch pieces

6 satay sticks

Mint Chutney (page 95), to serve

Method

1 Heat one teaspoon of oil in a non-stick pan and roast the gram flour on low heat till fragrant.

2 Place the yogurt, cumin powder, peppercorns, dried fenugreek leaves, turmeric powder, *garam masala* powder, lemon juice, salt and saffron in a bowl and mix well.

3 Add the roasted gram flour and mix well. Add the cottage cheese cubes and toss gently. Set aside to marinate for ten to fifteen minutes.

4 Thread the ingredients in the following order onto the satay sticks: onion, cottage cheese, green capsicum, red capsicum, cottage cheese, onion.

5 Heat a shallow non-stick pan; add the remaining oil and place the satay sticks on it. Cook on medium heat, turning the satay sticks from time to time so that the cottage cheese pieces are cooked evenly all around.

6 Serve hot with mint chutney.

TAWA PANEER CHAAT

Ingredients

500 grams cottage cheese,
cut into ½-inch pieces

Crisp puffed *puri* (as for
paani puri), as required

1½ tablespoons oil

2 large onions, chopped

1 teaspoon ginger paste

1 teaspoon garlic paste

3-4 green chillies, seeded
and chopped

¾ cup tomato purée

3-4 tablespoons *pav bhaji masala*

Salt to taste

½ tablespoon *chaat masala*

2-3 tablespoons chopped
fresh coriander

Method

1 Heat the oil on a non-stick *tawa*; add
the onions and sauté till brown. Add
the ginger paste and garlic paste and
continue to sauté for a few minutes.

2 Add a little water and continue to
sauté for one minute. Add the green
chillies and sauté for another minute.

3 Add the tomato purée, *pav bhaji masala*, salt and *chaat masala* and continue to cook over low heat till the oil separates from the *masala*.

4 Add the cottage cheese and half the chopped coriander and stir gently to mix. Check seasoning and cook over low heat for two minutes.

5 Make a hole in each *puri* and stuff with the cottage cheese mixture.

6 Serve, garnished with the remaining chopped coriander.

PANEER FRANKIES

Ingredients

150 grams cottage cheese, crumbled

1 cup wholewheat flour

Salt to taste

1 tablespoon oil + for shallow-frying

1 large onion, roughly chopped

1 large tomato, chopped

1 teaspoon ginger paste

1 teaspoon garlic paste

¼ teaspoon Kashmiri chilli powder

¼ teaspoon turmeric powder

1 teaspoon coriander powder
(optional)

1 tablespoon lemon juice

4 teaspoons Green Chutney (page 95)

1 medium onion, finely chopped

Chaat masala, as required

Method

1 Mix together the wholewheat flour and salt, with sufficient water and knead into a firm dough. Cover with a damp cloth and set aside for about fifteen minutes.

2 Heat one tablespoon oil in a non-stick pan; add the onion, tomato, ginger paste, garlic paste, salt, chilli powder, turmeric powder and coriander powder, and stir well. Cook till soft and pulpy and the excess moisture has dried up.

3 Add the cottage cheese and lemon juice; stir and take the pan off the heat. Divide the filling into four equal portions and set aside. Divide the dough into four equal balls and roll out into thin *roti*.

4 Heat a non-stick *tawa*, place a *roti* on it, drizzle a little oil all around and cook till both sides are evenly cooked.

5 Spread a teaspoon of green chutney over each *roti*. Place a portion of cottage cheese mixture at one end. Sprinkle some onion and *chaat masala* over the filling and roll up the *roti*.

6 Wrap in aluminum foil or greaseproof paper and serve.

Note: For a non-vegetarian version, replace cottage cheese with boneless chicken cubes. Add the chicken to the onion-tomato *masala* and cook till tender.

HARE MASALE KA BHUNA PANEER

Ingredients

- 8 one-inch cottage cheese cubes
- 1 large tomato, cut into 1-inch cubes
- 1 medium green capsicum, cut into 1-inch cubes
- 1 medium red onion, cut into 1-inch cubes
- 5 tablespoons melted butter
- 1 tablespoon lemon juice
- 2 teaspoons *chaat masala*

- ½ tablespoon chopped ginger
- 10 garlic cloves
- 6 green chillies, chopped

Paste

- 1 cup fresh coriander leaves
- ½ cup fresh mint leaves
- 2 tablespoons pomegranate kernels

First Marinade

- 1 tablespoon ginger paste
- 1 tablespoon garlic paste
- 2 tablespoons lemon juice
- 1 teaspoon salt

Second Marinade

- 1 cup drained yogurt
- ½ teaspoon salt

- ½ teaspoons *garam masala* powder

- 2 teaspoons cumin powder

- 4 tablespoons gram flour, roasted (see Chef's Tip)

- 1 tablespoon dried fenugreek leaves, powdered

- 1 tablespoon filtered mustard oil

- 10 curry leaves

Method

1 Dip the coriander leaves and mint leaves for one minute in hot water and immediately strain into a colander. Wash under running tap water for thirty seconds and allow to drain for thirty minutes. Place the coriander leaves and mint leaves with the pomegranate kernels, ginger, garlic and chillies in a blender. Blend into a paste with two tablespoons water. Transfer to a bowl. Set aside.

2 To make the first marinade, place the ginger paste and garlic paste in a bowl and combine well with lemon juice and salt. Add the cottage cheese pieces and mix lightly. Marinate for thirty minutes.

3 To make the second marinade, mix together yogurt, salt, *garam masala* powder, cumin powder, gram flour and powdered dried fenugreek leaves in a deep bowl. To this add the coriander-mint paste. Combine well.

4 Pour the mustard oil in a small and deep non-stick pan and place on low heat. Tear the curry leaves into small bits with hand. As the oil begins to smoke, add the curry leaves and immediately take the pan off the heat. Pour the seasoned oil into the second marinade.

Snacks

5 Add the cottage cheese along with the first marinade to the second marinade. Add the tomato, capsicum and onion and mix well.

6 Cover the bowl with a cling film and place it in the refrigerator to marinate for three to four hours.

7 Just before serving, thread the cottage cheese alternately with the tomato, capsicum and onion onto the skewers.

8 Place the skewers under a hot grill or place in a preheated oven at 220°C/425°F/Gas Mark 7 for three to four minutes. Take the skewers out and baste with two tablespoons of melted butter. Place them again under the heat for two to three minutes more.

9 Pour three tablespoons of melted butter into a non-stick frying pan and place on medium heat.

10 Remove the grilled cottage cheese and vegetables from the skewers and add to the hot butter. Stir-fry for thirty seconds on high heat.

11 Transfer into a serving bowl and sprinkle with lemon juice and *chaat masala*.

12 Serve immediately.

CHEF'S TIP

To roast gram flour, place a small non-stick pan on medium heat and add the gram flour. Roast, stirring continuously, till the gram flour is fragrant and turns a light brown in colour.

PANEER TIKKA KALI MIRCH

Ingredients

500 grams cottage cheese,
cut into 1-inch cubes

12-15 black peppercorns

4 tablespoons oil

2 tablespoons gram flour

¼ teaspoon carom seeds

1 tablespoon ginger-garlic paste

1 teaspoon green chilli paste

1 cup drained (hung) yogurt

3 tablespoons fresh cream

Salt to taste

½ teaspoon *garam masala* powder

¼ teaspoon green cardamom powder

¼ teaspoon turmeric powder

1 medium green capsicum,
cut into 1-inch pieces

Butter for basting

Method

1 Dry-roast the peppercorns and crush to a coarse powder. Set aside.

2 Heat two tablespoons oil in a non-stick *kadai* and sauté the gram flour and carom seeds for two to three minutes on low heat.

 Snacks

3 Transfer to a bowl and set aside to cool. Add the ginger-garlic paste, green chilli paste, drained yogurt, fresh cream, salt, *garam masala* powder, green cardamom powder and the crushed peppercorns and mix well.

4 Heat the remaining oil in a small non-stick pan; add the turmeric powder and immediately add this to the mixture in the bowl.

5 Mix well, add the cottage cheese cubes and capsicum pieces and mix gently. Set aside to marinate for one hour preferably in a refrigerator.

6 Thread the cottage cheese cubes and capsicum pieces alternately onto a skewer and grill for five to six minutes, basting occasionally with butter.

7 Serve hot with onion rings and Mint Chutney (page 95).

PANEER TIKKA KATHI ROLL

Ingredients

Paneer Tikka Filling

- 1 cup cottage cheese, cut into ½-inch cubes
- 2 medium tomatoes, seeded and chopped
- 2 teaspoons oil
- 2 medium green capsicums, seeded and chopped

Marinade

- ¼ cup yogurt, whisked
- 1 teaspoon red chilli powder
- ¼ teaspoon turmeric powder
- ½ teaspoon ginger paste

- ¼ teaspoon garlic paste
- 1 tablespoon gram flour
- ½ teaspoon *chaat masala*
- ½ teaspoon dried fenugreek leaves
- ½ teaspoon *garam masala* powder
- Salt to taste

Chapati

- 1 cup wholewheat flour
- ¼ cup milk
- Salt to taste

 Snacks

Method

1 Mix together all the ingredients of the marinade in a deep bowl. Add cottage cheese and tomatoes and toss lightly. Set aside to marinate for ten minutes.

2 Heat oil in a non-stick pan. Add green capsicums and sauté for two minutes.

3 Add the cottage cheese mixture and sauté over high heat for four to five minutes, stirring occasionally. Cook till dry and set aside.

4 For *chapati,* combine all the ingredients and knead into soft dough. Divide the dough into eight equal portions. Roll out each portion into a thin *chapati*.

5 Heat a non-stick *tawa* and cook each *chapati* lightly on both sides. Set aside.

6 Divide the cottage cheese *tikka* filling into eight equal portions.

7 Place one portion of the filling in the centre of each *chapati* and roll up tightly.

8 When you want to serve, cook the rolls on a hot *tawa* till they get warmed up. Cut into two-inch long pieces and serve hot.

GRILLED PANEER WITH HONEY-CHILLI SAUCE

Ingredients

- 400 grams cottage cheese, cut into fingers
- 2 tablespoons butter

Masala Paste

- 3-4 dried red chillies
- 1 teaspoon coriander seeds
- ½ teaspoon cumin seeds
- 3-4 peppercorns
- ½ inch cinnamon
- 3 cloves
- A pinch of nutmeg powder
- 1 tablespoon oil
- 1 teaspoon ginger paste
- 1 teaspoon garlic paste

Sauce

- 2 tablespoons oil
- 8-10 garlic cloves, crushed
- 1 medium onion, chopped
- 1 teaspoon red chilli flakes
- 1 tablespoon soy sauce

2 tablespoons honey

1 tablespoon cornflour

Salt to taste

¼ teaspoon pepper powder

Method

1 For the *masala* paste, dry-roast the dried red chillies, coriander seeds, cumin seeds, peppercorns, cinnamon, cloves and nutmeg on a non-stick *tawa* and grind to a coarse powder.

2 To the powder add the oil, ginger paste and garlic paste and mix well.

3 Heat a non-stick *tawa*; add the butter and roast the cottage cheese till it attains nice brown colour on all sides.

4 You can achieve the same results in a sandwich toaster.

5 For the sauce, heat the oil in a non-stick pan, add the crushed garlic and stir for half a minute.

6 Add the chopped onion, red chilli flakes, prepared *masala*, soy sauce and honey and stir for a few minutes.

7 Add the cornflour mixed in one-fourth cup of water. Bring to a boil and cook until the sauce thickens. Season with salt and pepper.

8 Serve the grilled cottage cheese accompanied with honey-chilli sauce.

CHILLI-PANEER

Ingredients

- 6-8 green chillies, stemmed and sliced
- 300 grams cottage cheese, cut into 1-inch fingers
- 3 tablespoons cornflour
- 2 tablespoons oil + for deep-frying
- 3-4 garlic cloves, peeled and crushed
- 1 medium red onion, thickly sliced
- 2 medium green capsicums, seeded, cut into thick strips
- 1 cup Vegetable Stock (page 95)
- ¾ teaspoon salt
- 2 tablespoons soy sauce

Method

1 Place the cottage cheese fingers in a bowl and sprinkle one tablespoon cornflour. Toss well so that the cottage cheese fingers are well coated with the cornflour.

2 Heat sufficient oil in a non-stick *kadai* and deep-fry the cottage cheese fingers for one minute or until the edges start to turn brown. Drain on an absorbent paper.

3 Place the remaining cornflour in a small bowl and add half cup of water. Whisk well. Set aside.

4 Heat two tablespoons oil in another non-stick pan and sauté the garlic for thirty seconds.

5 Add the onion, capsicums and chillies and continue to sauté for two to three minutes.

6 Add the cottage cheese and stir in the vegetable stock. Add the salt and soy sauce and stir.

7 Add the cornflour mixture and cook on high heat, stirring, till the sauce is thick enough to coat the cottage cheese and the vegetables and take off the heat.

8 Serve hot immediately.

LEHSUNI PANEER TIKKA

Ingredients

850 grams cottage cheese, cut into 1½-inch cubes

2 tablespoons garlic paste

2 tablespoons *tandoori masala*

300 grams drained (hung) yogurt

3½ tablespoons fresh cream

5-6 garlic cloves, chopped

1 green chilli, chopped

2 tablespoons chopped fresh coriander

Salt to taste

1 tablespoon red chilli powder

½ tablespoon turmeric powder

1½ tablespoons *garam masala* powder

1 tablespoon carom seed powder

1 tablespoon *chaat masala*

4 tablespoons roasted gram flour (page 26)

1 tablespoon vinegar

2 tablespoons oil

Method

1 Slit the cottage cheese cubes without cutting through. Mix one tablespoon of the garlic paste and *tandoori masala* in a small bowl. Stuff the mixture into the slit cottage cheese cubes. Set aside.

2 Mix together the yogurt, cream, remaining garlic paste, the chopped garlic, green chilli, fresh coriander, salt, chilli powder, turmeric powder, *garam masala* powder, carom seed powder, *chaat masala*, roasted gram flour, vinegar and oil in a bowl.

3 Marinate the stuffed cottage cheese cubes in the marinade for around two hours in a refrigerator.

4 Preheat an oven to 200ºC/400ºF/Gas Mark 6.

5 Thread the cottage cheese cubes, one-inch apart, onto the skewers. Cook the cottage cheese in the preheated oven for eight to ten minutes, or roast or grill over live charcoal or in a *tandoor* over a moderate heat for six to eight minutes.

6 Serve hot with salad and Green Chutney (page 95).

 Snacks

PANEER TIKKA MASALA

Ingredients

500 grams cottage cheese, cut into 1-inch cubes

2 medium green capsicums, cut into 1-inch pieces

2 tablespoons oil

1 tablespoon butter

Marinade

1 cup drained yogurt

1 tablespoon ginger paste

1 tablespoon garlic paste

2 teaspoons Kashmiri red chilli powder

1 teaspoon *garam masala* powder

2 tablespoons lemon juice

Salt to taste

1 tablespoon mustard oil

Onion-Tomato Masala

1½ tablespoons oil

1 teaspoon cumin seeds

4 medium onions, chopped

7-8 garlic cloves, chopped

1 teaspoon ginger paste

- 1 teaspoon garlic paste
- 3 large tomatoes, chopped
- Salt to taste
- ¼ cup tomato purée
- 1½ tablespoons red chilli powder
- ¼ teaspoon turmeric powder
- 1 teaspoon coriander powder
- 1 teaspoon cumin powder
- 1 tablespoon chopped fresh coriander
- 1 teaspoon crushed dried fenugreek leaves
- 1 teaspoon *garam masala* powder
- ¼ cup cream

Method

1 To make the *tikka*, combine together all the ingredients for the marinade and whisk well. Dip the cottage cheese cubes in the marinade and set aside to marinate for half an hour, preferably in the refrigerator.

2 Thread the marinated cottage cheese cubes onto skewers. Heat the oil on a non-stick *tawa* and place the skewers on it. Cook, turning the skewers a few times, so that the cottage cheese brown evenly on all sides. Take the cottage cheese cubes off the skewers, place on a plate and set aside.

3 For the onion-tomato *masala*, heat the oil in a non-stick pan. Add the cumin seeds and when they begin to change colour, add the onions and sauté till well browned. Add the garlic and sauté till

lightly browned. Add the ginger paste and garlic paste, and continue to sauté for another minute.

4 Add the tomatoes and salt and cook, covered over low heat till the tomatoes are soft and pulpy.

5 Add the tomato purée, chilli powder, turmeric powder, coriander powder, cumin powder and half a cup of water and cook, covered, over medium heat for three to four minutes, or till the oil separates.

6 Stir in the fresh coriander, dried fenugreek leaves, *garam masala* powder and cream. Cook for another two minutes.

7 Add the cottage cheese *tikka* and capsicum, stir gently and serve with a dollop of butter on top.

PANEER PASANDA

Ingredients

400 grams cottage cheese

2 large onions, quartered

1½ inches ginger

10 garlic cloves

20 cashew nuts

15-20 raisins, chopped

½ teaspoon white pepper powder
Salt to taste

½ cup cornflour

1 tablespoon oil + for deep-frying

1 bay leaf

4-5 cloves

1 inch cinnamon

4-5 green cardamoms

6-8 black peppercorns

3 green chillies, finely chopped

1 teaspoon red chilli powder

¼ teaspoon turmeric powder

1 teaspoon coriander powder

2 cups tomato purée

1 teaspoon green cardamom powder

1 tablespoon sugar

½ cup fresh cream

Method

1 Mash a quarter of the cottage cheese, and cut the rest into one-and-a-half-inch squares of one-fourth-inch thickness. Set aside.

2 Boil the onions in half a cup of water. Drain and grind to a fine paste. Set aside.

3 Finely chop half-an-inch of ginger. Grind the remaining ginger and the garlic to a fine paste. Set aside.

4 Soak half the cashew nuts in half a cup of warm water for fifteen minutes. Drain and grind to a paste. Chop the remaining cashew nuts.

5 Mix together the mashed cottage cheese, chopped ginger, chopped cashew nuts, raisins, white pepper powder and salt. Sandwich the mixture between two slices of cottage cheese.

 Main Dishes

6 Make a thick batter of the cornflour, salt and water.

7 Heat sufficient oil in a non-stick *kadai*; dip the stuffed cottage cheese in the batter and deep-fry till crisp and golden. Drain on absorbent paper. Set aside.

8 Heat one tablespoon of oil in a non-stick *kadai*. Add the bay leaf, cloves, cinnamon, cardamoms and peppercorns and sauté till fragrant. Stir in the boiled onion paste and cook for two minutes.

9 Add the green chillies, ginger-garlic paste, chilli powder, turmeric powder and coriander powder and cook for one minute.

10 Add the tomato purée and bring to a boil. Stir in the cashew nut paste mixed with a little water. Cook for five minutes, stirring continuously. Add the salt and cardamom powder.

11 Add one cup of water and sugar and bring to a boil. Add the fried cottage cheese and fresh cream, and stir gently to mix. Serve hot.

PANEER MAKHNI

Ingredients

- 350 grams cottage cheese, cut into 1-inch triangles
- 1 cup butter
- 2 tablespoons oil
- 12 green cardamoms
- ½ blade of mace
- 20 garlic cloves, roughly chopped with the skin
- 2½ teaspoons red chilli powder
- 18 large tomatoes, roughly chopped
- 1¾ teaspoons salt
- 2 teaspoons roasted powdered dried fenugreek leaves
- 3 teaspoons honey
- 8 tablespoons fresh cream

Method

1 Heat two tablespoons of oil in a non-stick pan and sauté the cardamom and mace for one minute or till fragrant. Add the garlic and sauté for one minute.

2 Mix the chilli powder in three tablespoons of water to make a paste.

3 Add this paste to the pan and continue to sauté for thirty seconds.

4 Add the tomatoes and salt and cook for fifteen minutes or till the tomatoes turn pulpy. Strain this mixture through a strainer into a deep non-stick pan.

5 Transfer the residue into a blender jar and grind to a smooth paste. Pass this through the strainer and add this to the strained liquid. Add three-fourth cup of water and stir well.

6 Place a non-stick *tawa* on medium heat and place the pan with the gravy over it. Add the butter and simmer the mixture, stirring occasionally, for ten minutes or till the raw flavours of tomato disappear.

7 Add the powdered dried fenugreek leaves and honey. Stir and cook for five minutes more. Add the cream and cook for two minutes more.

8 Add the cottage cheese and stir gently.

9 Serve hot with *naan* or *parantha*.

POTATO CHEESE BALLS IN SPINACH GRAVY

Ingredients

2 medium potatoes,
boiled and mashed

200 grams cottage cheese, mashed

3 tablespoons cornflour

½ teaspoon red chilli powder

½ inch ginger, chopped

Salt to taste

½ teaspoon white pepper powder

12-15 cashew nuts, chopped

12-15 raisins

Oil for deep-frying

Spinach Gravy

2 medium bunches (350 grams each)
fresh spinach leaves

2 green chillies, chopped

3 tablespoons oil

½ teaspoon caraway seeds

5-6 garlic cloves, chopped

½ cup tomato purée

½ teaspoon turmeric powder

1 teaspoon coriander powder

Salt to taste

1 teaspoon *garam masala* powder

¼ cup cream

Method

1 Mix together the mashed cottage cheese and potatoes, cornflour, chilli powder, ginger, salt and white pepper powder.

2 Divide the mixture into sixteen balls. Stuff each ball with cashew nuts and raisins.

3 Heat plenty of oil in a non-stick *kadai* and deep-fry the balls, a few at a time, until golden brown. Drain on absorbent paper and set aside.

4 For the gravy, blanch the spinach in plenty of water; refresh under cold running water and drain well. Blend with the green chillies to a smooth purée.

5 Heat three tablespoons of oil in a non-stick *handi*; add the caraway and garlic and stir-fry for a few minutes. Add the spinach purée and cook for about two to three minutes. Stir in the tomato purée and mix well.

6 Add the turmeric powder, coriander powder and salt. Stir and cook for four to five minutes.

7 Add one cup of water and bring to a boil. Lower heat and simmer for five to seven minutes.

8 Stir in the *garam masala* powder and cook till the curry is reduced by half. Lower heat, stir in the cream and cook for half a minute. Remove from heat.

9 Arrange the *kofte* in a serving dish. Pour the hot gravy over and serve hot.

CHANAR DALNA

Ingredients

250 grams cottage cheese,
    cut into ½-inch cubes

  2 medium potatoes, cut into
    ½-inch cubes

1½ teaspoons cumin seeds

  1 teaspoon red chilli powder

 ½ teaspoon turmeric powder

  1 inch ginger, roughly chopped

    Oil for deep-frying

 ½ tablespoon ghee

2-3 green chillies, slit

  1 teaspoon *garam masala* powder

 ½ teaspoon sugar

    Salt to taste

 ½ cup milk

Method

1 Grind together one teaspoon cumin
seeds, chilli powder, turmeric powder,
ginger with little water to a fine paste.

2 Heat sufficient oil in a non-stick *kadai*
and deep-fry the potatoes till light
golden brown. Drain on absorbent paper
and set aside.

 Main Dishes

3 Heat the ghee in a non-stick pan, add the remaining cumin seeds and when they begin to change colour add the *masala* paste and cook for two minutes stirring continuously.

4 Add the potatoes, green chillies, *garam masala* powder, sugar and salt and half a cup of water, cover and cook for three to five minutes.

5 Mix in the milk and allow it to simmer for another two to three minutes. Add the cottage cheese to the potato gravy. Stir and simmer for a minute.

6 Serve hot.

PANEER PISTE KA SALAN

Ingredients

- 500 grams cottage cheese
- 150 grams pistachios, blanched and peeled
- 2 cups oil
- 2 large red onions, peeled and sliced
- ½ cup plain yogurt
- 4 tablespoons Mint Chutney (page 95)
- 1 tablespoon garlic paste
- ½ tablespoon ginger paste
- 2 tablespoons pure ghee
- 5 green cardamoms
- 5 cloves
- 1 inch cinnamon
- 2 mace blades
- 7-8 saffron threads, crushed
- ½ teaspoon *garam masala* powder
- A pinch of mace powder
- 2 teaspoons salt
- 2-3 drops screw pine water

Method

1 Heat the oil in a non-stick *kadai* and fry half the sliced onions till the onion turns brown. Drain and place on an absorbent paper.

2 Place a small non-stick pan on medium heat and pour in two cups of water and bring it to a boil. Add the pistachios and cook for two minutes. Strain, cool and peel.

3 Place the pistachios in a blender jar, reserving one tablespoon for garnishing. Add the remaining sliced onion, two tablespoons browned onions and yogurt and grind to a smooth paste. Transfer to a bowl.

4 Cut the cottage cheese into triangles with each side measuring one-inch. Place them in a bowl and add the green chutney and stir lightly.

5 Cover the bowl with a lid and set aside to marinate for fifteen minutes.

6 Place the garlic paste and ginger paste in a small bowl, add two tablespoons of water and stir well. Set aside.

7 Place a non-stick pan on medium heat and pour in one tablespoon ghee. When it melts, add the cardamoms, cloves, cinnamon and mace and sauté for thirty seconds or till fragrant.

8 Add the diluted garlic-ginger paste and sauté for fifteen seconds. Add the pistachio paste, stir and cover the pan with a lid. Simmer for two to three minutes.

9 Add the saffron, *garam masala* powder, mace powder, salt and one cup of water and simmer for four to five minutes.

10 Heat the remaining ghee in another non-stick frying pan on medium heat and add the marinated cottage cheese in it and sauté over high heat for two minutes, stirring gently so that the cottage cheese pieces do not break.

11 Transfer the cottage cheese pieces into a serving dish.

12 Add the screw pine water to the simmering pistachio gravy and stir. Take the pan off the heat and pour the gravy immediately over the cottage cheese pieces.

13 Serve hot garnished with the reserved pistachios and the remaining browned onions.

PANEER BHURJI

Ingredients

400	grams cottage cheese
1½	tablespoons oil
2	teaspoons cumin seeds
3-4	green chillies, slit
4	medium onions, chopped
½	teaspoon turmeric powder
½	teaspoon red chilli powder
	Salt to taste
2	tablespoons chopped fresh coriander

Method

1 Heat the oil in a non-stick pan; add the cumin seeds and green chillies. When the seeds begin to change colour, add the onions and sauté till light brown.

2 Add the turmeric powder, chilli powder and salt, and stir well to mix.

3 Crumble the cottage cheese and add to the pan and mix well. Cook for two to three minutes, stirring lightly.

4 Serve hot, garnished with the chopped coriander.

SHAHI PANEER

Ingredients

- 400 grams cottage cheese
- 6 medium tomatoes, roughly chopped
- 2 large red onions, peeled and quartered
- 2 tablespoons oil
- 3 cloves
- 2 one-inch cinnamon sticks
- 1 bay leaf
- 2 green chillies, stemmed and slit
- 1 teaspoon fresh ginger paste
- 1 teaspoon fresh garlic paste
- 1 teaspoon Kashmiri red chilli powder
- 2 teaspoons coriander powder
- ½ teaspoon turmeric powder
- ½ teaspoon black pepper powder
- ¼ cup cashew nut paste
- 1 cup fresh cream

  A pinch of saffron
- ½ teaspoon *garam masala* powder
- 1 teaspoon salt
- ¼ teaspoon green cardamom powder

Method

1 Place the tomatoes in a blender jar and grind to a smooth purée. It will give you around two cups of purée.

2 Cut the cottage cheese into half-inch wide and one-inch long pieces.

3 Place a small non-stick pan on medium heat and add half a cup of water. Add the onion and boil them for five to seven minutes. Take the pan off the heat and drain off the excess water. Allow the boiled onions to cool. Place in a spice grinder and grind to a fine paste. Transfer into a bowl.

4 Heat the oil in a non-stick pan and sauté the cloves, cinnamon and bay leaf for thirty seconds or till fragrant.

5 Add the chillies and boiled onion paste and reduce the heat to low. Sauté for three to four minutes so that it does not get coloured. Add the ginger paste and garlic paste and continue to sauté for thirty seconds.

6 Add the tomato purée and sauté for five to seven minutes or till the oil surfaces. Add the chilli powder, coriander powder, turmeric and pepper powder and sauté for one minute.

7 Add the cashew nut paste and sauté for another two minutes. Stir in the cream, saffron and *garam masala* powder, one teaspoon salt and one cup water. Stir well and let it come to a boil. Simmer for three minutes.

8 Add the cottage cheese and stir gently. Sprinkle with green cardamom powder and serve hot.

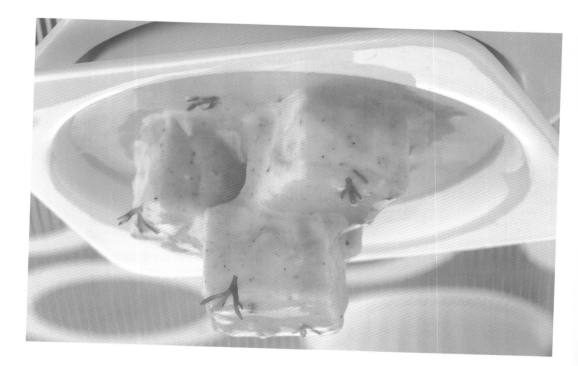

PANEER KALIYA

Ingredients

- 500 grams cottage cheese, cut into 1-inch cubes
- ½ cup almonds, blanched, peeled and ground
- 1 tablespoon pure ghee
- 4 green cardamoms
- 4 cloves
- 10 black peppercorns
- 1 inch cinnamon
- 2 medium onions, sliced
- 1 inch ginger, chopped
- 2 tablespoons coriander seeds
- ½ teaspoon turmeric powder
- Salt to taste
- 2 tablespoons chopped fresh coriander

Method

1 Heat half a tablespoon of ghee in a non-stick *kadai*.

2 Crush the cardamoms, cloves and peppercorns with a mortar and pestle and add to the ghee. Add the cinnamon and onions and sauté for two to three minutes.

Paneer Kaliya

 Main Dishes

3 Add the ginger and coriander seeds and sauté for a minute longer. Remove from heat, cool slightly and grind into a fine paste with one tablespoon of water.

4 Heat the remaining ghee in the same *kadai*; add the ground *masala* paste and sauté until the ghee separates. Add one tablespoon of water to prevent scorching.

5 Mix the almond paste with one cup of water and add to the *masala*. Add the turmeric powder and simmer for a while. Add salt to taste and mix well.

6 Add the cottage cheese cubes and simmer for ten minutes. Serve hot, garnished with chopped coriander.

PANEER JHALFREZI

Ingredients

- 300 grams cottage cheese, cut into 1-inch fingers
- 2 medium tomatoes, halved and seeded
- 2 medium green capsicums, halved and seeded
- 2 medium onions, thickly sliced
- 1 tablespoon olive oil
- 1 teaspoon cumin seeds
- 2 dried red chillies, halved
- 1 inch ginger, cut into thin strips
- 1–2 green chillies, chopped
- 1 teaspoon red chilli powder
- ½ teaspoon turmeric powder
- Salt to taste
- 1½ tablespoons vinegar
- 1 teaspoon *garam masala* powder
- 1 tablespoon chopped fresh coriander

Method

1 Cut the tomatoes and capsicums into thick slices. Separate the layers of the sliced onions.

2 Heat the oil in a non-stick *kadai*. Add the cumin seeds. When they change colour add the red chillies, ginger strips, green chillies and onions. Sauté for thirty seconds.

3 Stir in the chilli powder and turmeric powder. Add the capsicums and cook for two-three minutes. Add the cottage cheese and toss.

4 Add the salt and vinegar and cook for two to three minutes. Stir in the tomato pieces and *garam masala* powder and cook for two minutes.

5 Garnish with chopped coriander and serve hot.

METHI CHAMAN

Ingredients

- 350 grams fresh fenugreek leaves, chopped
- 150 grams cottage cheese, cut into ½-inch cubes
- ¼ teaspoon turmeric powder
- 1 teaspoon red chilli powder
- 1 cup buttermilk
- 2 tablespoons ghee
- ½ teaspoon caraway seeds
- 3-4 garlic cloves, finely chopped
- 350 grams spinach , chopped
- ¼ teaspoon dried ginger powder
- ¼ teaspoon green cardamom powder
- ¼ teaspoon white pepper powder
- Salt to taste

Method

1 Blanch the fenugreek leaves. Drain and squeeze to remove excess water.

2 Mix the turmeric powder and chilli powder with the buttermilk.

3 Heat the ghee in a non-stick *kadai*; sauté the cottage cheese cubes to a golden brown and drain on absorbent paper.

 Main Dishes

4 In the same ghee, add the caraway seeds and stir-fry for ten seconds. Add the garlic and sauté till light brown. Add the spinach and sauté for five minutes.

5 Add the fenugreek leaves and stir-fry for three to four minutes. Add the buttermilk and mix. Cook for another two to three minutes.

6 Add the cottage cheese and mix. Sprinkle dried ginger powder, cardamom powder, white pepper powder and salt, and stir-fry for two minutes.

7 Serve hot with rice.

PANEER TAMATAR KA KHUT

Ingredients

250 grams cottage cheese,
   cut into 1-inch fingers

15 medium tomatoes, chopped

½ lemon-sized ball tamarind

2 inches ginger, peeled
   and chopped

10-12 garlic cloves, crushed

6-8 dried red chillies, stemmed
   and broken into 2 pieces

1 tablespoon sesame oil

1 teaspoon mustard seeds

1 teaspoon cumin seeds

20 curry leaves

3 one-inch cinnamon sticks

1 teaspoon turmeric powder

2 teaspoons coriander powder

1 teaspoon roasted
   cumin powder

1½ teaspoons salt

2 tablespoons roasted
   Bengal gram, powdered

½ cup coconut milk

Method

1 Take a deep bowl and soak the tamarind in one cup of warm water for thirty minutes. Squeeze out the pulp, strain and set aside.

2 Place a deep non-stick pan over medium heat and add half cup of water, the tomatoes, ginger, garlic and chillies and bring to a boil.

3 Reduce the heat to low, cover the pan with a lid and simmer for twenty to twenty-five minutes, or till the tomatoes become pulpy. Take pan off the heat and set aside to cool.

4 Pass the cooled mixture through a soup strainer and set aside in a bowl. Transfer the residue into a blender jar and grind to a smooth paste. Pass this through a strainer into the same bowl.

5 Heat the sesame oil in a non-stick pan; add the mustard seeds and cumin seeds and sauté till the mustard seeds begin to splutter.

6 Add the curry leaves, cinnamon, turmeric powder, coriander powder and cumin powder and sauté for one minute.

7 Add the prepared tomato mixture and bring to a boil. Stir in the tamarind pulp and the salt.

8 Add the powdered roasted Bengal gram and stir thoroughly.

9 Reduce the heat to low and stir in the coconut milk and cottage cheese. Simmer for two to three minutes and take the pan off the heat. Serve hot with *parantha*.

PANEER BABY CORN BALCHAO

Ingredients

- ½ kg cottage cheese
- 7-8 baby corn cobs
- 10-12 whole red chillies
- 1 inch ginger, roughly chopped
- 8-10 garlic cloves , roughly chopped
- 1 teaspoon cumin seeds
- 7-8 cloves
- 1 teaspoon mustard seeds
- 1 inch cinnamon
- Salt to taste
- ½ cup malt vinegar

- 1 tablespoon oil
- 2 medium onions, chopped
- 2 medium tomatoes, chopped
- ¾ cup tomato purée
- 1 teaspoon sugar

Method

1 Wash and cut the cottage cheese into diamond shaped pieces. Wash the baby corn cobs and boil them in sufficient water for two to three minutes. Drain and cut into small pieces.

2 Grind the whole red chillies, garlic, ginger, cumin seeds, cloves, mustard seeds, cinnamon and salt with a one-fourth cup of malt vinegar to a fine paste.

3 Heat the oil in a non-stick pan, add the onions and sauté till light brown. Add the tomatoes and mix. Cook for five minutes, stirring well.

4 Add the baby corn, tomato purée and ground *masala*.

5 Cook for three to four minutes. Add the sugar, adjust salt and mix well.

6 Add the cottage cheese pieces and the remaining malt vinegar. Cook for five to seven minutes. Serve hot.

METHI TAMATAR PANEER

Ingredients

250 grams fresh fenugreek leaves

4 medium tomatoes, finely chopped

200 grams cottage cheese, cut into ½-inch cubes

2-3 green chillies

1 inch ginger

6 garlic cloves

1 tablespoon oil

- 2 medium onions, finely chopped
- 1 tablespoon Kashmiri red chilli powder
- 1 tablespoon coriander powder
- Salt to taste
- 1 teaspoon dried mango powder

Method

1 Grind together, the green chillies, ginger and garlic to a paste.

2 Heat the oil in a non-stick pan; add the onions and sauté for three to four minutes or till they just start turning brown.

3 Add the ginger-garlic-green chilli paste, stir-fry for a few seconds and add the chilli powder, coriander powder and salt to taste. Mix well.

4 Immediately, add the chopped fenugreek and cook on medium heat, stirring continuously for six to eight minutes, or until completely cooked and dry.

5 Add the tomatoes, stir and cook over high heat for two to three minutes. Add half a cup of water, cover and simmer for three to four minutes.

6 Add the cottage cheese; sprinkle dried mango powder and mix well.

7 Cook till the cottage cheese is heated through, and serve immediately.

PUDINA PANEER PULAO

Ingredients

- 100 grams cottage cheese, cut into 1-inch cubes
- ½ cup roughly chopped fresh mint
- 1¾ cups Basmati rice
- 2 green chillies, roughly chopped
- 1½ inches ginger, roughly chopped
- ¾ cup yogurt, whisked
- 2 tablespoons ghee
- 2 bay leaves
- 4-6 green cardamoms
- 4-6 cloves
- 2-3 black cardamoms
- 8-10 black peppercorns
- Salt to taste

Method

1 Soak the rice in three cups of water for half an hour and drain.

2 Grind the mint leaves, green chillies, ginger and yogurt into a smooth chutney.

3 Heat the ghee in a thick-bottomed non-stick pan.

4 Add the bay leaves, green cardamoms, cloves, black cardamoms and

peppercorns. When they begin to sizzle, add the mint chutney and cook for two to three minutes.

5 Add two and three-fourth cups of water and bring to a boil. Stir in salt to taste.

6 Add the drained rice and bring to a boil.

7 Cover the pan and cook over low heat for about eight to ten minutes, or till the rice is completely cooked.

8 Gently stir in the cottage cheese and serve hot.

TIRANGA KOFTA PULAO

Ingredients

- 1½ cups Basmati rice, soaked
- 3 tablespoons ghee
- 3 small onions, sliced
- Salt to taste

Paneer Kofta

- 150 grams cottage cheese, grated
- Salt to taste
- ¼ teaspoon white pepper powder
- ½ teaspoon green cardamom powder
- 1½ tablespoons cornflour
- Oil for deep-frying

Green Rice

- 200 grams spinach
- 1 green chilli
- 2 garlic cloves

White Rice

- 1 teaspoon cumin seeds

Yellow Rice

- A few saffron threads

Method

1 Mix the cottage cheese with the salt, white pepper powder and cardamom powder, and mash well.

2 Divide into eighteen equal portions and shape into balls. Dust with cornflour.

3 Heat sufficient oil in a non-stick *kadai* and deep-fry the cottage cheese balls till golden brown. Drain on absorbent paper.

4 Boil the rice in four cups of water till almost done; drain. Divide into three equal portions.

5 For the green rice, blanch the spinach in plenty of water.

6 Drain and purée in a blender along with the green chilli and garlic.

7 Heat one tablespoon of ghee in a non-stick pan; add one-third of the onions and sauté till translucent.

8 Add the spinach purée and sauté for one minute over high heat. Add one part of the rice along with six cottage cheese balls and salt, and toss to mix. Transfer to a bowl and set aside.

9 For the white rice, heat one tablespoon of ghee in a pan; add the cumin seeds and when they begin to change colour, add half the remaining onions and sauté till translucent.

10 Add another part of the rice, six cottage cheese balls and salt, and toss well. Transfer to a separate bowl and set aside.

11 For the yellow rice, soak the saffron in two tablespoons of water. Heat one tablespoon of ghee in a non-stick pan, add the remaining onions and sauté till translucent.

12 Add the remaining rice with the saffron water. Add the remaining cottage cheese balls and salt, and toss to mix. Transfer to a bowl and set aside.

13 To serve, in a transparent square glass dish, spread a layer of green rice and level the surface.

14 Spread a layer of white rice over the green rice and level the surface. Top with a layer of yellow rice.

15 Alternatively, arrange the rice in a pattern on a flat dish.

CHANAR PULAO

Ingredients

- 400 grams cottage cheese, cut into 1-inch cubes
- 1½ cups Basmati rice
- 1½ tablespoons ghee
- 2 teaspoons sugar
- 1 large onion, finely sliced
- 1 bay leaf
- 1 inch cinnamon
- 2 cloves
- 2 green cardamoms
- Salt to taste

Method

1 Wash and drain the rice and spread out to dry. When completely dry, add half a tablespoon of ghee and the sugar, and mix well.

2 Heat half a tablespoon of ghee in a non-stick pan and sauté the cottage cheese cubes on medium heat. Drain and set aside.

3 Add the remaining ghee to the same pan and sauté the onion on medium heat till crisp and brown. Drain and set aside.

4 To the ghee remaining in the pan, add the bay leaf, cinnamon, cloves and

 Rice

cardamoms, and sauté till fragrant. Add the rice and salt, and sauté for two or three minutes.

5 Add three cups of hot water and bring to a boil. Lower heat, cover and cook till the rice is tender and all the water has been absorbed.

6 Add the cottage cheese cubes and stir lightly to mix. Sprinkle the fried onions and serve.

PANEER PEAS PULAO

Ingredients

400 grams cottage cheese, cut into 1-inch cubes

½ cup shelled green peas, blanched

1½ cups Basmati rice

3 tablespoons ghee

2 teaspoons sugar

1 large red onion, peeled and finely sliced

1 bay leaf

1 inch cinnamon

2 cloves

2 green cardamoms

2½ teaspoons salt

Method

1 Wash and drain the rice and spread out to dry on an absorbent towel. When completely dry, transfer into a deep bowl and stir in one tablespoon of ghee and sugar.

2 Place a small non-stick pan on medium heat and pour in one tablespoon of ghee. When the ghee melts, add the cottage cheese cubes and toss them so that they are evenly browned on all the sides. Drain and set aside.

3 In another non-stick pan, add the remaining ghee and add the onion and place it on medium heat. Sauté for two to three minutes or till the onions are crisp and brown. Drain and set aside.

4 To the ghee remaining in the pan, add the bay leaf, cinnamon, cloves and cardamoms and sauté for thirty seconds or till fragrant. Add the rice and salt and sauté for two to three minutes.

5 Add three cups of hot water and bring to a boil. Reduce the heat, cover the pan with a lid and cook for eight to ten minutes or till the rice is done and all the water has been absorbed.

6 Add the cottage cheese cubes and green peas and stir lightly. Sprinkle the browned onions and serve immediately.

Rice

SANDESH

Ingredients

8 cups (1.6 litres) milk

¼ cup lemon juice

½ cup (65 grams) caster sugar

A pinch of green cardamom powder

12 pistachios, blanched and finely chopped

Method

1 Bring the milk to a boil in a deep, thick-bottomed non-stick pan. Add the lemon juice and stir till the milk curdles. Strain and immediately refresh the *chhena* in chilled water.

2 Put the *chhena* in a piece of muslin and squeeze till all the water is drained out.

3 Knead the *chhena* well with the heel of your hand. Add the caster sugar and cardamom powder, and knead again.

4 Cook in a non-stick pan on medium heat for eight minutes. Remove from heat and divide into twelve equal portions. Roll each portion into a ball and make a dent on the top.

5 When cooled, place a pistachio in the dent and serve.

Makes 12 sandesh/350 grams

CHHENA MURKI

Ingredients

250 grams cottage cheese,
cut into ½-inch cubes

1 cup (250 grams) sugar

1 tablespoon milk

2-3 drops screw pine essence

Icing sugar, for dusting

Method

1 For the syrup, cook the sugar with one cup of water, stirring continuously, till the sugar dissolves. Add the milk. Collect the scum, which rises to the surface with a ladle, and discard. Cook the syrup till it attains a one-string consistency.

2 Add the cottage cheese and cook till the syrup coats the cubes well.

3 Remove from heat, add the screw pine essence and mix well. Keep swirling the pan till the cubes are thickly coated with the syrup and separated from each other.

4 Arrange in a serving plate and sprinkle liberally with icing sugar.

Makes 300 grams

Note: The shelf life of cottage cheese is short, so consume *chhena murki* as soon as possible.

 Mithai

CHUM CHUM

Ingredients

Chhena

- 10 cups (2 litres) cow's milk
- 8 teaspoons (40 ml) white vinegar
- 1 tablespoon refined flour
- ½ teaspoon cornflour

Syrup

- 4⁴/₅ cups (1.2 kg) sugar
- 2 tablespoons milk

Topping

- 2 tablespoons (40 grams) *khoya/mawa*
- 1 teaspoon rose water

- 3-4 saffron threads
- 1 tablespoon sugar syrup
- A small pinch or a few drops of edible yellow colour

Method

1 Boil the milk on high heat. Set aside to cool slightly (77°C/170°F).

2 Mix the vinegar in one and three-fourth cups of water and add to the hot milk. Stir lightly till the milk curdles. Add three to four cups of cold water and a few ice cubes and stir. Strain the *chhena* through a piece of muslin and squeeze to

remove all the water. You should have 250 grams of *chhena*. Transfer the *chhena* onto a worktop. Mix together half a teaspoon of refined flour and the cornflour, and add to the *chhena*. Knead with the heel of your hands to a smooth mixture.

3 Divide the mixture into twenty-five equal portions and roll into oblong smooth rolls, taking care that there are no cracks. Make a small dent on one side and set aside. Mix the remaining flour with half a cup of water and set aside.

4 To make the syrup, cook the sugar with five cups of water, stirring continuously till the sugar dissolves. Add the milk and let the syrup come to a boil. Collect the scum, which rises to the surface, with a ladle and discard. Continue to cook the syrup for a few minutes longer. Strain the syrup into a bowl. Pour one cup of the syrup into a deep, wide non-stick pan and add four to five cups of water. When the syrup comes to a boil, add the *chhena* rolls and half the flour-water mixture. The syrup will start frothing. Let the rolls cook in the syrup. Do not stir, but gently agitate the syrup so that the balls do not stick to the bottom of the pan.

5 Slowly drizzle half a cup of water along the sides of the pan every five minutes to prevent the syrup from thickening and forming strings. Continue cooking for fifteen minutes, or till the rolls spring back to their original shape. Drain the rolls and soak in the reserved syrup. Chill for at least two hours so that the syrup is absorbed by the *chhena* rolls.

6 For the topping, cook the *khoya* with the rose water, saffron, sugar syrup and yellow colour till the mixture thickens to the consistency of jam. Take the *chhena* balls out of the syrup, spread a little of the *khoya* mixture into the hollows and serve.

Makes 25 chum chum

Mithai

KHEER KADAM

Ingredients

- 16 mini *rosogulla*
- 2 cups + 3 tablespoons (420 grams) *khoya/mawa*
- 4 tablespoons powdered sugar
- ½ teaspoon rose essence

Method

1 Squeeze the mini *rosogulla* to remove excess sugar syrup. Grate two cups of *khoya* finely. Add the powdered sugar and knead into a smooth dough.

2 Place a non-stick frying pan on high heat; add the *khoya*-sugar mixture and sauté for four to five minutes. Transfer to a bowl and set aside to cool.

3 When cool, add the rose essence and knead well. Divide the *khoya* mixture into sixteen equal portions and shape into balls. Make small hollows in the centre with your thumb. Thin the edges and place a mini *rosogulla* in each hollow.

4 Cover the *rosogulla* completely with the *khoya* so that no part of it is left exposed. Roll once again into balls. Grind the remaining *khoya* to a powder. Roll the balls in the powdered *khoya*. Store in a refrigerator and serve chilled.

Makes 16 kheer kadam/400 grams

Note: As *kheer kadam* contains *chhena* and *khoya*, it does not have a long shelf life. They should be consumed at the earliest.

RAJ BHOG

Ingredients

Chhena

    10 cups (2 litres) cow's milk

    8 teaspoons white vinegar

    1 tablespoon refined flour

    ½ teaspoon cornflour

Filling

    ¼ cup (45 grams) *khoya/mawa*

    1 tablespoon pistachios

    ⅛ teaspoon green cardamom powder

    A few saffron threads

    ¼ teaspoon rose water

Syrup

    4⁴/₅ cups (1.2 kg) sugar

    2 tablespoons milk

    A few saffron threads

    A few drops of yellow food colour

Method

1 Bring the milk to a boil over high heat. Set aside to cool slightly to 77°C/170°F.

2 Mix the vinegar in one and three-fourth cups of water and add to the hot milk. Stir lightly till the milk curdles. Add

Raj Bhog

 Mithai

three to four cups of water and a few ice cubes and stir.

3 Strain the *chhena* through a piece of muslin and squeeze to remove all the water. You should have 250 grams of *chhena*.

4 Transfer the *chhena* onto a worktop. Mix together half a teaspoon of refined flour and the cornflour, and add to the *chhena*. Knead, pressing with the heel of your hand, till the mixture is smooth.

5 Divide into twenty-five equal portions and roll into balls.

6 For the filling, grind together, the *khoya*, pistachios, cardamom powder, saffron and rose water coarsely. Divide into twenty-five equal portions and roll into small balls.

7 Stuff each *chhena* ball with a portion of the filling and roll again into a ball taking care that no cracks form.

8 Mix the remaining refined flour with half a cup of water and set aside.

9 To make the syrup, cook the sugar with five cups of water, stirring continuously till the sugar dissolves. Add the milk and let the syrup come to a boil. Collect the scum, which rises to the surface with a ladle, and discard. Continue to cook the syrup for a few minutes longer. Strain the syrup into a bowl.

10 Pour one cup of the syrup, reserving the rest, into a deep and wide non-stick pan and add four to five cups of water. When the syrup begins to boil add the *raj bhog*. Add half the flour-water mixture - the syrup will start frothing. Cook

the *raj bhog*, gently agitating the syrup so that the balls do not stick to the bottom of the pan.

11 Slowly drizzle half a cup of water along the sides of the pan every five minutes so that the syrup does not thicken. Continue cooking for fifteen minutes or till the *raj bhog* spring back when pressed. This is a sign that they are cooked.

12 Add the saffron and yellow colour to the reserved syrup.

13 Remove the *raj bhog* from the cooking syrup with a slotted spoon and place in the saffron-flavoured syrup. Chill for at least two hours till the *raj bhog* absorb the syrup. Serve.

Makes 25 raj bhog/1 kg

🌿 Mithai

MALAI SANDWICH

Ingredients

Chhena

2 litres cow's milk

8 teaspoons (40 ml) white vinegar

1 tablespoon refined flour

½ teaspoon cornflour

Syrup

4⅘ cups (1.2 kg) sugar

2 tablespoons milk

Filling

2 tablespoons (30 grams) *khoya/mawa*

1 teaspoon rose water

3-4 saffron threads

1 tablespoon sugar syrup

A small pinch or a few drops of yellow food colour

Method

1 Bring the milk to a boil on high heat. Set aside to cool slightly to about 77° C/170°F.

2 Mix the vinegar in one and three-fourth cups of water and add to the hot milk. Stir lightly till the milk curdles. Add

three to four cups of water and a few ice cubes and stir.

3 Strain the *chhena* through a piece of muslin and squeeze to remove the excess whey. You should have 250 grams of *chhena*.

4 Transfer the *chhena* onto a worktop. Mix together half a teaspoon of refined flour and the cornflour, and add to the *chhena*. Knead, pressing with the heel of your hand, till the mixture is absolutely smooth.

5 Divide into twelve equal portions and shape into squares, taking care that there are no cracks.

6 Mix the remaining refined flour with half a cup of water and set aside.

7 To make the syrup, cook the sugar with five cups of water, stirring continuously till the sugar dissolves. Add the milk and bring the syrup to a boil. Collect the scum, which rises to the surface with a ladle, and discard. Continue to cook the syrup for a few minutes longer. Strain the syrup into a bowl.

8 Pour one cup of strained syrup, reserving the rest, into a deep, wide non-stick pan; add four to five cups of water and bring to a boil. Add the *chhena* squares and half the flour mixture. The syrup will start frothing. Let the *chhena* squares cook. Do not stir but just agitate the syrup gently so that the squares do not stick to the bottom of the pan.

9 Slowly drizzle half a cup of water along the sides of the pan every five minutes so that the syrup does not thicken.

Continue cooking for fifteen minutes longer, or till the *chhena* squares spring back when pressed. This is a sign that they are cooked.

10 Remove the *chhena* squares with a slotted spoon and place in the reserved syrup to soak. Place in a refrigerator to chill for at least two hours, or till the *chhena* squares absorb the syrup.

11 In a separate non-stick pan, cook the *khoya*, rose water, saffron, sugar syrup and yellow colour together till the mixture attains the consistency of jam. Divide the mixture into twelve equal portions.

12 Remove the *malai* squares from the syrup, slit each in half horizontally. Spread the *khoya* mixture on one half, place the other half over it and serve.

Makes 750 grams

BASIC RECIPES

Green Chutney
Grind together 1 cup fresh coriander, ½ cup fresh mint, 2-3 green chillies, black salt to taste, ¼ teaspoon sugar and 1 tablespoon lemon juice to a smooth paste using a little water if required.

Mint Chutney
Grind 5 cups mint leaves, 3 cups coriander leaves, 10 green chillies, 3 onions, and 3 inches of ginger to a fine paste, adding a little water if required. Stir in 1 tablespoon lemon juice, salt and pomegranate seed powder to taste.

Vegetable Stock
Peel, wash and chop 1 onion, ½ medium carrot, 2-3 inch celery stalk and 2-3 garlic cloves. Place in a non-stick pan with 1 bay leaf, 5-6 peppercorns, 2-3 cloves and 5 cups of water and bring to a boil. Lower heat and simmer for 15 minutes and strain. Cool and store in a refrigerator till further use.

GLOSSARY

English	Hindi	English	Hindi
Capsicum	Shimla mirch	Mace	Javitri
Cardamom	Elaichi	Nutmeg	Jaiphal
Carom seeds	Ajwain	Pistachio	Pista
Cashew nuts	Kaju	Raisins	Kishmish
Cinnamon	Dalchini	Refined flour	Maida
Cottage cheese	Paneer	Saffron	Kesar
Dried fenugreek leaves	Kasoori methi	Screw pine	Kewra
Dried red chillies	Sookhi lal mirch	Semolina	Rawa/sooji
Fresh cream	Malai	Spinach	Palak
Fresh mint	Pudina	White vinegar	Safed sirka
Gram flour	Besan		